2/22

WAKING

Phoenix Poets

A SERIES EDITED BY ROBERT VON HALLBERG

TOM SLEIGH

WAKING

THE UNIVERSITY OF CHICAGO PRESS

Chicago and London

Tom Sleigh teaches in the English Department at Dartmouth College.
Among his many honors are an Ingram Merrill Foundation Grant,
a National Endowment for the Arts Fellowship, and a John Simon
Guggenheim Memorial Fellowship.

The University of Chicago Press, Chicago 60637
The University of Chicago Press, Ltd., London
© 1990 by The University of Chicago
All rights reserved. Published 1990
Printed in the United States of America

99 98 97 96 95 94 93 92 91 90   54321

Library of Congress Cataloging-in-Publication Data

Sleigh, Tom.
    Waking / Tom Sleigh.
        p.   cm. — (Phoenix poets)
    ISBN 0-226-76238-6 (alk. paper).—ISBN 0-226-76239-4 (pbk. :
    alk. paper)
    I. Title.   II. Series.
    PS3569.L36W3   1990
    811'.54—dc20   90-31100
                                                      CIP

For Tim, Jay,
and Ellen

Contents

Acknowledgments

Grateful acknowledgment is made to the following magazines in which many of these poems first appeared:

Agni: "Afterwords," "Ending."
Antaeus: "Don't Go to the Barn."
The Boston Review: "The Porch Swing," "A Vision," "Sunday Drive."
Grand Street: "Fish Story."
The Paris Review: "The Last Word," "Vows."
Ploughshares: "Hope," "Last Wish," "Elk at Black Fork Canyon."
Pequod: "The Physical," "Intelligence."
Poetry: "Animus," "The Seal," "The Root Cellar" (under the title "First Love"), "M. on Her Thirtieth Birthday," "On the Seventh Floor: Cancer Ward."
Raritan: "In June," "'Dear Customer.'"
Shenandoah: "You Have Her Eyes."
Western Humanities Review: "Marché aux Oiseaux," "Stone."
The Yale Review: "Aubade."

I would also like to thank the John Simon Guggenheim Foundation, the National Endowment for the Arts, and the Ingram Merrill Foundation for their generous support.

Finally I would like to express my deep gratitude to F. B., R. P., S. H., A. G., A. S., A. M., S. B., M. A., S. Q., D. G., and M. H. for their criticism and encouragement.

one

Waking

Near that hour of the dawn when the swallow
Begins to sadly sing, remembering
Perhaps the pain of her past sorrows,
And when our mind like a pilgrim
Journeys farther from the flesh, less hemmed in
By pressing thoughts, so that in its vision
It seems almost divine, I saw as in a dream
An eagle with golden feathers hovering
In the air, its spread wings ready to swoop down.
And it seemed that I was there in that selfsame
Place where Ganymede was snatched from his companions
And borne up to that highest of high thrones.
And my thoughts spoke inside me: "Perhaps this valley
Is that flowering ground, the sole place chosen
For the scornful bird to strike its prey,
And carry it off, clutched in its proud talons."
And after circling and circling, it seemed to blaze
Down upon me terrible as lightning
And transport me to the heights of the sphere of fire:
There we seemed to burn together
As a single flame, and that imagined blaze
So singed me that it broke my slumber.

from Dante, *Purgatorio,* ix

Ending

When I first learned
I went home to lie down.
The fear in me took me by the throat.
What I had wished for—

      that my life
Would be a hook, and the hook a paradigm
Of suffering I could not escape, suffering
Whose knowledge would be impossible to bear
Even as I braced and kept bracing
To bear it—

   had been granted.

       Until then I had loathed
My safety—

   now I saw disaster

In the hanging baskets of fuchsias, the fig tree
Littering the yard with leaves, the staghorn ferns
Thrusting into the air, the eucalyptus strewing scaly bark
Like shed skin, in the intolerable, unlivable
Eden of my mother's garden . . .

She put out her hand
To rest it on my shoulder
                    and I stiffened as if I had been stung.

—My heartbeat throbbed in my ears
And I was drunk with looking at her face
That was transfigured, the eyes brimming with a light
That reduced me to the fluoroscopic
Beauty of an x-ray:
                    I was dying.

To know that I was dying seemed to perfect
Each moment—
                    the patio, cool, well-watered

Among the neighbors' cool, well-watered gardens,
Garden giving on to garden in the spiral
Of streets spiraling out
Around each other in an oasis
Of cool, well-watered gardens
                    bounded by the heaving,

Salt desert of the Pacific and the stark shining
Of the inland light carving around
The houses an aura that was desolate and throbbed
With the cleanliness of the desert—
                    an aura gripping

The city, molding it to a cold
Pinprick of light

                    that was my face, my mother's
Face, the neighbors' faces, that was the face

Of a child staring out from behind a mask,
The face frozen but for the shifting of the eyes . . .

I saw her eyes implore me
As though by giving her my life
She could protect me from my death

—My death that surrounded me,
As I lay in my mother's garden, cool, well-watered,
Immensely calm.

       . . . .

NO SMOKING NO EXIT FOLLOW THE RED LINE

After a day of routine tests, of walking round and round,
I sat in the waiting room, anxious to go home;

The light fell on my hands, on the plastic
Chairs and walls, and the room
Blurred to a shimmer,
                everything transfigured

To the poverty of its form

So that the old man in his shabby coat,
His hat clutched in his hands, twisting and worrying
And crumpling the brim
As he stood speaking to the receptionist

Seemed to lose identity,
            his face expressionless
As the white exhausted face of his waiting wife
Staring absently past her magazine
Down the neon-bleached corridor.

He bowed his head, his deferential
Nod and perfect manners
Making him somehow helpless, more helpless than she
In her bathrobe and bedroom slippers.

Sitting back down to wait, he nervously
Clutched her hand
                              as she stared past him

To the window, her glazed
Eyes unwavering as if hypnotized by sunlight

Which seemed to speak the world—
                              vocables

Of trees and cloud submerging
In the glare, impenetrable, dazing
As her faceless reverie . . .

Reflected in the glass my face
Flickered between theirs as I moved
Nearer to the window and sat shivering
In the cool sunlight, terrified
                              yet strangely glad

To think that this was hell

And that hell was to be between two worlds,
The anonymous facelessness of death
And his nervous, clutching hand . . .

The light washed across the pane, a light
Whose unceasing glare flooded through the room
Until the plastic of my chair
                              by its bare touch
Seemed all that held me:

My doctor's predictions, my parents'
Grimfaced concern, my friends' tight-lipped,
Failing smiles, my own fragile counsel
That really I was not so different,
After all, one misstep in the street—

                                    torn free
From habit, lost in the glare scouring
The pane, I leaned forward
Into that light, a space empty and whirling

As when I'd fainted in the street
Three months after I had learned, my heart
Pounding so fast that I felt deafened

When I woke, my body cold in the dim light
Suffusing the emergency room
Where beyond the curtain drawn around my bed

I heard a voice mutter that she'd
Stabbed herself with scissors, stabbed herself
In her own womb—

                        and then a muffled gasping, words
Wrenched from deep inside

                        —"*Quiero morir, morir*"—

Pierced through the curtain
On which her shadow blankly writhed, her head
Rolling side to side as her teeth snapped
At the doctor's hands
                                        to please, please let her die

Until his shadow rose above her and strapped her down,
Wrapped loops of gauze around her wrists, and tied them to the bedframe .

The hypodermic plunged in my arm

And I shivered and repeated
With the insistence of a prayer,
"My temperature is a 104, 104, 104 . . ."

                                        Was this
What it meant to die? —

Numbness unfolding in my brain, my skull
Splitting to the darkness pouring in, the ooze and float
Of prickling flesh drifting from beneath the cool
White sheet
                    and lifting me up into a fog
Of neon where I hovered

High above her pain, and looked down
To where their shadows churned, wrestling hugely
Across the curtain
                            behind which their voices twined,
Hers a wrenched, muffled groan,
                                        his brutal, chopping, hard:

"Unless I operate
                    you'll die—" "*Quiero morir,*
                                        morir,

Morir—" "You'll die, damn it,
                        I'm saying you'll die."

The neon winced and dripped and burned,
The steel bars of the trolley rattling
As they wheeled her off down the corridor;
                            tears stung my eyes

And I don't know why, for I was glad she said
Just what she said, that I want to die, *morir,* to die . . .

—At last the receptionist called my name
And I followed the technician to the x-ray room:

Left alone in the dark, bare to the waist,
I spread my arms and embraced the machine,
Listening to the insect chuckle and click
Gnawing me down to a skeleton . . .

I shut my eyes and saw in the dark
The light flickering across the room, our faces
Burning in the windowpane, the coffee
Steaming in the sun—
                        and then I heard her voice
Whispering, "*Quiero morir, morir, morir . . .*"

                                and heard beneath it
My own breath rising
Unstoppably among the ripped magazines
And the windows like dungeons of reflections . . .

The indeterminate faces flickering and vanishing
Concealed in the glare between two worlds.

　　　　　　. . . . . . .

The morning after my aunt's funeral
Seems etched in that cool sunlight which pierced
My mother's garden, the flowers bending
　　　　　　　　　　　　to her hands blotched
With liver spots and crepe lines, the flesh
Puffy around the knuckles
As she held the watering can, the water,
Clear and glancing, gathering to fall—

And yet as if that sunlight were a wall, my mother and I
Talking there just six months ago
Seem unreachable behind the glare, unreal
　　　　　　　　　　　　as the blur
Of hummingbirds
Darting between the flowers.

It is only when I recall her voice
Talking of my aunt's death, of her senile
Confusion as she smeared herself with her own shit
And smiled and sang "just like Ophelia,"
Do I recognize myself,
　　　　　　　　still untouched by the knowledge
Of my sickness, but sensing in my aunt's suffering

That no scattered lilies or scarlet flowers,
No passage through the Gates of Sleep, no vision
Of the Underworld, of Grief, pale Disease,
Want, Age, Dread, and avenging Care

                                        would redeem
The poverty of her dying
And lead her into the ease of the Blessed Groves . . .

As I listen to my mother's voice
Hovering among uncertainties, I hear her words,
"The cruelest thing is to live beyond your time——",
As if it were leave to die,
                              a leave she couldn't know
She gave, until, as in a dream, I found myself
A few months later in the same ward where my aunt
Had died . . .

                    Again my mother's hand
Brushes back the leaves, and I see reflected
In her pupils my face as in a curving mirror
As if only in her calm gray eyes could I exist
Among her flowers, the broad, overhanging leaves——

Until sunlight washing through the fig tree
Doused the flicker of my face, so that lost
In that green shade and dark swirl of my mother's
Voice,
          "To be waiting and not even to know
That you are waiting . . .",
                              I felt my aunt's

Presence in the sudden flooding glare——
And saw her raised expectant eyes, her hand
Weakly lifting to shade
Her gaze——
              and then she vanished into the shadows
And was nothing but my mother's voice talking,
                                        her absence

Irremediable, but my memory insisting
She was there as if hidden in the leaves,
The glare like a burning door swinging open
To a room where I would see her face to face—

                                as if to meet her gaze
With unflinching eyes while she lay there in her nightgown
Waiting, was a trust, a dark promise, a binding act
Of love . . .

            And yet having met that stare,
I hear my mother's voice as though the words were mine
Obliged to give up the dying to the dead:

"A week before she passed away,
They began giving her morphine. Her eyes
Got glassy but her wrinkles smoothed
When the pain eased
                    and her face seemed almost young—
Drawn and white, but younger than I'd ever seen . . .

She was so thin her nightgown kept sliding
Off her shoulders
                and I remember how before she fell
She would strip naked in the street and yell,
'Come on, boys, I'm ready for you . . .'

                            and then she smiled,
A clear wide smile that I recalled from photographs
When she was a girl—
                    seeing what she was, so wasted,
So frail, it was mercy
That she couldn't see that smile—
                            she sat there

Staring into space, her nightgown bunched
Around her waist, her skin shining like a child's
After fever:
                    She seemed so utterly a stranger

That it frightened me to look at her—
                                        I kept
Wanting to touch her, but I didn't dare
Disturb that smile:

                    Her name; who she'd been;
The sour odor off her skin—none of that
Seemed real:
                    Only that smile;

Though what her smile meant or means now,
If it meant more than muscle stretched on bone . . .
Perhaps she was happy;
Or happy, at least, to die . . .

                              And so I smiled back
And she nodded as if to thank me, as if my smile
Gave her permission—

And then the nurse came in to change her chuck."

As we stood there, lapped and lapped
In that green shade,
                    above my mother's head
The windchime's lazy ringing
Was like a sunlit stillness welling from
The flowers, from the fronds of the mimosa
Curling into balls and the tangled bougainvillea
That smelled of rising heat.

The windchime
Swayed in the clear air
And I felt a weight like an anchor
Plunging through me as through deep water,
And then a stillness that was the blindness
Of sunlight pressed against my face, the furnace of

Bougainvillea glowing scarlet through the glare;
And then I smelled the lilies, faintly sour in the calm,
And watched the bones of my mother's hand
Shift slightly beneath the skin
As she tipped the spout of the watering can
And poured the water out into the air.

        .   .   .   .   .   .

When my mother comes to visit me
At home or in the hospital, she is shocked
To see how thin I am—
                    as if between us the past
Was a kind of body, a set of memories, mutual obligations
That my body once contained . . .

Sometimes I think I have two bodies,
One young and strong, the other that of an old man,
And my self—
            my memories, thoughts, sensations—

Lives between the two bodies,
Divided, unreconciled to my change;

And as if I'd dreamed the habits of my health,
The pills, shots, and tests
                    that the old man undergoes
So weaken the young man's body that his pain

Negates our past, says only
In answer to her questioning look
That the continuity of our shared memories is broken
By my body's change . . .

And though I tell myself that who *I* am
Is not so different,
                              yet I can't ignore the way,
The last time she came to visit,

                              her eyes gazing
From the bedroom mirror pretended to stare
Past me, straining not to see:

                              The light that she'd
Switched on melted my nakedness
In the glass to a smear of burning white
So that as I turned I saw an invalid, frail, gaunt-ribbed,
Shrunken to a skeleton:

                              Captive in the mirror,
As if to breathe would break the glass, I held my breath
Back in my lungs—
                              and saw a face

Floating behind my face, pale and luminous as
It drifted, nestling and gently freezing
To the hollows of my skull, its underwater eyes
Drowned deep in the sockets staring up
As through dark water at a world
Beyond the glass:

Immersed in that face's looking,
I saw through those eyes the utter stranger
That I had become—
                    and knew with a cool shock

That the face behind my face, its eyes gazing
Back at me with hypnotized
Disinterest, unagonized and childlike,
Was the face of my own death . . .

After we had talked, my mother rose
To leave, and with pained, secret courtesy,
As if unwilling that I should see that face
Which she had pretended not to see,

                              when I turned
Toward the mirror and saw our reflections
Hovering there,
                    my mother turned out
The light—
                but before her touch could find me,
I saw our two faces, buoyed up
By the dark, floating there, pale, cool, the eyes
Distant in the mirror affirming
What we knew, but didn't dare to say:

                                    I held
My mother's hand, and watched our faces
Floating there, the eyes steady, unflinching,
Staring through us from the darkness of the glass.

                    . . . .

My doctor tells me I am lucky,
That someone in my condition lives more intensely;
That if my condition grows stable
I could live a long time—

                      but then he knits his brows,
Warning me to caution, that for reasons
As yet unknown—.
                But in this, he says,
I am no different from anyone,
Only closer to what most of us ignore . . .

When I step outside the examining room
To make a future appointment
The secretary treats me as just another patient;

But when I step into the street
My knowledge that I am no different
Is, in fact, my difference—
                    and rises like a wall

Between my body and my self; between my body
And the other lives passing in the street; between my body
And the body of the world . . .

                      Sometimes I see myself
As living outside my body, anterior to my body
As I study it from above, watching my arms lift,
My eyes blink, my forehead wrinkle—
                    can this stranger
Be that self whose name and date of birth
I saw illumined in my dream?

The night before I was released
From the same ward where my aunt died,
I dreamed that I had drowned:

                              Sunlight
Striking through the water
Played across my face, pale, featureless,
A blank reflector of that light—
                              I stared up through the water
Floating the leather-bound Bible
My aunt gave me when I was a child:

                              On the page marked
For births and deaths I saw her careful handwriting
Keep smearing and fading, the date
Of my birth, *November 28, 1953,*
                              an unintelligible
Swirl of ink drifting and drifting
Through the water . . .

                              I heard my aunt's voice
Telling me that I had drowned—

                              and then the ink
Coiled and looped to the letters
Of a foreign script, elaborate black knots
Which if only I could read them would restore
My aunt to life, explain each moment
Of her suffering—

But another voice, my mother's,
Began to argue with the letters, saying
That my aunt must stay dead, that the date
Of her death was inscribed in a Bible
                              and could not be changed . . .

As I lay there, my body numb and heavy,
I sensed beneath me
                        a shadow shearing
Slowly upward, circling and circling
Through the darker water

                            so that my need to
Read the letters, to see in my aunt's suffering
Some reason or a fate, seemed artificial, remote;

—And then my name, my mother's name, my dead and distant aunt's
Spelled themselves in the clumsy, sloping letters
Of a child,
                the names wrapping round me like a net
Which a hand that was my hand but from some place
Beyond the dream,
                        patiently lifted through the water—

I heard my mother's voice arguing
As a light shone on my face
From my name and date of birth lit up like neon—

But my body numb and heavy kept tearing
Through the mesh and drifting deeper down
Toward that power circling and circling . . .

When I woke the night-nurse was just leaving,
And I heard the heavy, harsh breath
Of the old man in the next bed as he sucked
Oxygen from the mask . . .
                                Down the corridor

Shadows from the nurses' station
Reared across the walls and floor:

My name, my mother's name, my dead and distant aunt's
Seemed strangely intermingled with the old man's breathing,
Each breath straining out of him,
                                        then sucked in
Hard and rasping, his grave face
Tranced in its wrinkles
                            staring into the shadows . . .

Through the window I could see the rushing headlights
Tunneling through the night
                                and beyond
The rising slopes of the darkened hills . . .

—And I thought to myself:
In a week I'll be thirty-three years old . . .

As I lay there intent on the rasping
Of his breathing, his chest beneath the sheet
Swelling and subsiding,
                            my lungs slowed to his

So that I heard in the intervals
Between that harsh sighing a silence
Underpinning the stillness of the ward:

I knew that he was dying,
That in a week he could be dead, his face
Slack beneath the mask, his body stiffening
Beneath the flimsy, washed-to-rags ward clothes . . .

And yet each swelling of our lungs
Seemed sustained by that dying, that gravid silence
Floating each low sound on the ward
                                        so that I heard

Each cough, each hushing, distant word
As if it were a promise unfolding with the world,
The terms exacting, unforeseeable, among
The bedpans and bedrails.

         · · · · · · ·

Today, my birthday, I felt well enough to walk
Through the mist drifting
Along the shore—
          and as if the waves were molten silver
Shining back to me my thoughts,
               I kept seeing
Bonnard's self-portrait
In which he paints

        his own reflection
In the bathroom mirror, his ribs sharp
Against the skin, eyes buried in the sockets,
Sunlight behind his bald head
Shining intolerably bright, a shuddering
Brilliance off the tiles walling him in—
            his gaze
Comprehends his own impending death, the deaths of his family
And oldest friends—
         yet the eyes captive in the glass

Stare undismayed by their own sadness
As if eyes behind the eyes staring
From a void of heart and thought
           saw his emaciated
Nakedness, the triumphant prominence of the bones,
As the world's
      frail, breathing ribs,
          his breath

Joined to the world's . . .

I sat down on a rock and listened to the waves'
Lap and shush,
                the sun glaring through the mist
Warm on my hands:

                   Was it his fate to paint
His own death, his skill at seeing
Turned on himself, his luck indistinguishable
From his suffering?

                 And yet this morning when I woke
To the foghorns calling across the water, the long notes
Woven and unwoven together, the only light a frost-scorched

Sunflower leaning up against the window,
Its immense pocked face like an eye
That never shuts, its stare
Staring through me as mine through it—

Free of all encumbrance, perfectly separate,
Yet culpable reflections of each other—
                        I knew

That as I lay there, and listened
To those long warning notes weaving through each other,

                                 that my luck
Lay in my fate; that, before I became ill, my longing
For a hook was, in fact, a kind of suffering:

As I sat there in the sunlight, the smell of salt
Rising damp and thick from the warming rock,
I seemed to hear again that laborious, harsh breathing,
To see my dying aunt stare

Into the glaring hospital lights, and my mother's
Hand reaching out to touch my shoulder—

All around me the mist, nestling, protective,
Began to slide and drift; the swell
Subsided, smoothed to crawling glass,
And in the lull between the breakers
I heard again the silence beneath the silence
Of the ward

     and sensed behind vapor
Wearing the sunlight like a mask
       that power
Shearing through dark water
Circling and circling . . .
      and as if it wore
My name, my mother's name, my dead and distant aunt's,
It seemed our lives hovered apart from us
And met suspended in that mist, featureless, bare:

Pure facelessness
     which turned from me
And hung in the blind distance, unraveling
Into the vacant, warming air.

two

Aubade

Lathe of the ocean. Perpetual
Motion machine of the waves. Everything still
Being turned and shaped to a shape nobody
Foresees: Ten years ago, was it, when we

Walked that shore, too earnest and sheepish
To hold hands? The wind cutting through our clothes
Cleansed and burned, the chill off the Atlantic
An ache we courted in our dumbstruck talk:

Callow, expectant, what wouldn't love give?
Cavalcanti's ray from Mars, Dante's wheel that moves
The planets and the stars, how nervous
We were, awkward and shivering: "Like this,

Do you like it like this?" Up all night,
Then waking to the smell of flannel and sweat,
We lay grateful, winded, goosefleshed in the chill,
Our own atmosphere rich and breathable:

We drank round the clock, embracing extremes,
Too hurried and heartsore to think of time . . .
Out fishing after midnight, we watched schools of squid
Slide and shimmer, tentacles tight-wrapped

Around our gig's hooks: Yanked from the water,
They spouted jets of ink, then pulsed and quivered
And faded to dead-white, their eyes, resigned and sober,
Opening wider and wider . . . Ten years more,

And will either of us remember
That ink sticky on our hands, the moon-glare
Rippling as we knelt underneath the pier
And scrubbed and scrubbed our hands in the dark water?

A Fable

She seems, almost, the hero in a fable,
Someone remote now, who once listened to him tell
The day's events before he asked her to tell;
Her hands around a coffee cup, she smiles
And sips in the once companionable silence
Which he now lives in by himself, still tranced
On those moments of compromise and need
When even arguments were understood
As a way to work to love, and be loved.
Theseus in the maze, Ariadne's thread,
She seems both together, a way in and out
Of these twisting corridors of thought
He searches in pursuit of a cause, a reason:
Why has it ended here, what could he have done
To make her happier, safer? The anger
At himself waits patiently, a monster
Contrite now, now that it's too late, who offers
Eagerly to let her cut its throat and swears
To do those things she no longer wants or asks:
Why has it ended up like this? The risks
They took together seem now a kind of fable,
Her version different from the one he tells.
Sitting there together, how distant she now is,

Her eyes serious as she tacitly refuses.
And even as he speaks, his words growing confused,
Foolish, desperate, a stranger in her maze
Of smiling stillness, he sees her side
Of things as clearly as his own: She slides
Her hand over his to keep him calm, her smile
Forgiving him the feelings he still feels.

Marché aux Oiseaux

I was in such a hurry I climbed
Two steps at a time, intent on seeing flowers,
Flowers cut for Sunday, stems shivering wet;
At the top of the stairs your hand almost slipped from mine

—Not flowers, but birds, pairs of birds in cages,
Nervous, enthralling, lighter-than-air creatures,
Their feathers ruffling up in rainbow-colored rages:
Wrong market, wrong day, wrong from the start!

Just like us, it somehow seemed, strangely met,
Blindly lucky in our chances . . . From some far-off tower
A bell, too serious, too loud, duly bonged the hour;
You bent down to a cage, eyeing a beak

Swiping cuttlebone, feathers blue and green
As your wide eye: To them is it all one
Whose future they become? Their vendor,
A fat man in suspenders, dozed in his chair,

Unwearyingly at home in the whistle, shriek, twitter—
A harem of both sexes, preening unconcerned,
Such topknotted vanity from plumes rising royally,
Arias wandering in and out of tune:

An opera wholly casual, telling a love story
Improvised and freshly staged day by day:
Each to his own cage, the singers seem to say!
Reflected in your gaze, they flock upward

Across your pupils, momentarily set free,
As my eyes fly to yours
And perch there quizzically: Better
Not to hide but to display

Our feathered finery! Two birds
Of a feather, our eyes lock together,
Our years, minutes, hours
Laid bare in your sharp-eyed stare!

In June

I

Figs we tear open looking for the worm,
The insides sticky, pearled with seed—
A harness hanging from a nail, whiff

Of engine oil, a scythe blade pocked
With rust. The ouzo bottles
Packed in straw, wrapped in faded newspaper

Shine clear as your eye
When you drink and clink your glass
With your fingernail, then run

A wet finger slowly round
The rim until the close shed rings
With a crystal hum.

II

The stars turn jittery
As night presses down.
The heat of the day
Off the whitewashed roof
Climbs my ankles to my knees

And cools. If only your hand
Rested lightly on my shoulder,
Or your arms were wrapped
Around my waist! The taste
Of iron is in the air,

Borne up from the fields
By the wavering heat: Rough-tongued in the dawn,
Always ready to go at it, our lovers'
Whiplash anthem, "I love you but . . . !"
And you climbing the steps now,

Skin goosebumped from your bath,
Your eyes' hard blue
Unflinchingly deliberate,
Wet lips stinging
Sweet from ouzo.

III

The cove rock
Hollowed and cratered
Like the moon
And the sea stretching bare
To the horizon.
Your face barely lifts
Above the foaming
Of the backwash
As you lie in the shallows
Half afloat, braced on your elbows,
Your head hanging back, eyes closed . . .

(The same look
Last night
When you groaned and sighed,
The sheets sticky,
Then cool, your throat's
Blue artery lightly throbbing . . .)

Even at this distance
I hold you close,
Water streaming off you
Like a negligee
As you rouse from the shallows
And wade out into the bay,
Dive and dissolve
Into a wave.

IV

Your song, off-key, melts and puddles
Into the blaze and blare of a motorbike
Climbing the slow, heat-rippled hill;

And later your sandals' scrape and clack, the mutter
Of fat drops from the wash dripping
On the stones, nervous as my fingers' drumroll:

I sat still as the cobweb in the corner,
My ears tuneless, tense, each nerve cocked,
Your shadow climbing the lamplit wall, your song's

Stillness rising up smothering and thick:
In the house across the way the crackle of oil frying,
Clank and clatter of silverware on plates;

Then hooves on cobbles, the donkey wheezing in his stall,
The pages of my book dully turning . . .
At last the small rustle of our sheets

Declaring the silence between us at a truce:
My fingers like the breeze wavering down your back;
My body pressed to yours, waterline to shoreline . . .

Then your sleeping breath unmoored, an island drifting.

Omen

The week after you had gone I woke
One morning, my eyes blurry from a night
Of ouzo and Homer, to convoys of trucks,
An armored car that lurched and roared, steel-skulled
As a dinosaur, while up from the tarmac
Heat waves reared and battled woozily
In the diesel-clogged air:
                                        Troy buzzed like a fly
Against the windowscreen, the radio
Sputtering with rumors of coup d'état:

Soldiers melted in the hilltop glare
Or crouched in ambush in an olive grove
—I thought of the bones from the massacres
Stacked in vitrines in the monastery chapel:
Femurs, scapulas, skulls crushed or neatly drilled
By a bullet hole . . .

                        Near noon I climbed the hill
To the outskirts of town and a tumbled-down wall
With a sign in tourist English, proper and strained,
"Here the Poet Homer Worked and Lived":
Toilet paper, condoms, a mosaic

Of broken glass, waste ground growing up to weeds,
The new moon an onion slip sprouting
From the sea—
                    and under my fingertips
The lichens on the stones, my touch reading
Them like braille, rough-tongued, upbraiding
As Achilles! . . .

              Meanwhile, the Greek navy
On maneuvers slicked the water black
As sunlight between the wall-stones wedged and pried;
My head ached as if I'd died and been brought back,
Each cell tingling and electrical—
Each whirlpooling dust-mote a charged particle.
I stood at attention, the light tensed
Above the sea raveling out in all directions
So that my eyes could find no place to hide,
No solid ground that didn't threaten to explode,
No grove or glade that wasn't boobytrapped
Or tripwired. Only you kept still, your absence
Shadowed by each rock and hill throbbing and wavering
In the heat . . .
                    A noon bell rang. Chickens squawked,
Wingbeats thudding dully as the neck
Snapped. Surging in my head the catalogue of ships,
The prows cutting water, the oars' flash and dip,
Made way for a destroyer—its radar shield
Idling, spinning round and round as it filled
The sluggish air with a throbbing whine,
Gray gun-turrets gleaming in the sun.

Home

Why, tonight, is the hot air
When it stirs her hand gliding
Across his cheek, and a girl's
Heady laughter rising from
The vacant lot to meet and meld
With the blare of some boy's
Radio, *their* two voices
Locked in argument? And when
Later he's drunk so much that
The faces she once put on
To show gratitude or fear
Float before him in a blur,
Does he try to embrace her
In his mind once again, though,
Supple as mist, she slides through
His embrace, a ghost in his
Underworld of losses: Like
Odysseus the wanderer
Down among the dead, he wants
To ask her where home is, that place
Marked out by their quarrels
And morning-after penitence;
But now the quiet warm place

Which is the whiskey calls to him,
Calls to him to sleep; and as
He lies down whirling, the whiskey
A slow wave that comes folding
Down around him and pulls him
Underwater to the stillness
Of the bottom, he hears echo
And throb beneath the radio's
Blare her voice calling all
Around him in the hot night air,
"Here, over here, *home* is here . . ."

"Dear Customer"

Cattails fraying and ragged weeds in a jar
Were meant to make your absence easier,
Less noticed than the influx
Of circulars and bills the post delivers,
Living dwindled down to selfless paper
That piles and clutters and gathers dust.

Love that could deliver as often disappoints
And leaves me to the mercy of my heart's own
Cramped compulsions, as if walls
Stripped bare in sun-furnished rooms reluctant
To be expansive or concede to me alone
Space that your presence once filled and made ample,

In their barrenness speak plainly my capacities.
Like fate I shrug and pick out less and less
The casual flicker of your eyes
That merge into the dazzle, unbearably
Bright, of routine life that lies
In a clutter on the desk: Faithfully

Arriving, unopened, anonymous.

Afterwords

The moon hugs the glass, a snail of phosphorus . . .
The dull "tick tock" of a manhole cover which the sleepless
Taxis rock back and forth sets echoing

—Remember!—that morning of hill on hill,
Terraces of mist burning off in the sun:
I lay in our room's high-raftered cool;

You bent to your bath, your face startling
Up from steam pluming off the surface
As settling in the water you began to wash,

The low lisp and mutter of drips and splashes
Drowned in the downpour when you rinsed. Eyes
Half-shut, abandoning your flesh to the buoyancy

Of water, you lay stretched out, shoulders
Goosefleshed, lipped by the slow ripples lifting
The lazy spreading tangles of your hair.

Half-conscious of my eyes when you climbed
From the water, your nakedness familiar,
Still wary of my touch, you drenched the tile floor,

Your hair a cloudburst when you shook it out
Then caught it up and wrapped it in a towel,
Your face half sunlit, half in shadow.

Bottle-green flies near the open shutters
Feinted and circled, then streaked through the window,
Their high-tension wire hum making us one ear

As the stillness rose up as from a well . . .
Late that afternoon, dry-throated, speechless,
We ambled down the lane, the tall cypresses

Like candles swooning in the sun. At a crossroads
We rested on a stump, the rings of grain
Swirling inward to a knot, the heartwood

We picked at dry and sapless, powdery to the touch
As we idly peeled strips of blistered bark.
At our feet the shade drew a dark

Circle, the sun's enormous roundness
Sluggishly molten swelling and swelling in
The heat-doused air. The fields sloped down

To ditches aswarm with larval flies, black clouds
Boiling above the ditch-banks. All the old
Questions slumbered in the heat, then roused

Like a black snake slithering across the road:
Last night's words barbed and edged, a foul-mouthed silence,
Our hurt smoldering between us in the bed

—And then above the swallows' slipknots and snares
We couldn't take our eyes from, their hunger
Unappeasable as they dipped and veered,

I sensed a lifting, an opening in air
Mellowed and clear: If only you were here,
Here to see us side by side sitting there,

Breathing in the simmer of far-off rain,
Smelling saltpeter in the lightning . . .
Sweat soaked through our shirts as the heat-haze cleared

And we tilted to dry lips a coldly sweating canteen,
Swallowing and swallowing great gulps of water
That tasted like iron or dew sucked from stones,

Heady as perfume as we dabbed it
On our wrists and behind our ears
And sprinkled it in each other's hair.

three

The Physical

Wrung out and clammy, my shirt stuck to my back
Against the seat's sweat-sour plush, the tires
Worrying in my ears as I looked
Out the bus window: HELL NO! WE WON'T GO!
Bled down a warehouse wall, but I was going
To my physical and, if they drafted me,
To the War. Subtly out of kilter, like a balance-scale's
Crossbeam, what was Right, what was Wrong
Seesawed sickly in my brain.
The silver sign above the windshield
DO NOT SPEAK TO THE CHAUFFEUR
Sanctioned our driver's silence, exempting
Him from confusion
As he sat square-shouldered, enthroned
In the glare rippling off the dew-slicked macadam.
My eyes slid down the aisle
To the other young men—how many, like me,
Let their fate ride on their number in the lottery?
Hand over hand the driver wrenched the wheel
As we streamed past schools
Of fuming, servile cars, groggy-eyed Jonahs
In the belly of the Whale: Dopers, greasers,
Brothers, straights, all of us plugged in

To that roaring heartbeat drowning out
Our separate motives and our fears . . .

"All right, Gentlemen, drop your drawers and cough;
Anybody for sure know they got a rupture?"
From test to test they'd herded us, the aides
Prodding us forward into long shuffling lines,
Our paper slippers rustling as we milled
Before the glassed-in booths that shielded
The tight-faced doctors:

                        Nerves raw
And prickling, palms chill
With sweat, I thought of putting on the helmet,
The camouflage-drab uniform and thick-soled
Shining boots, of squeezing the snug trigger
Of an M-16 . . . My mind's eye filmed
Over, the War that was larger, tougher, fiercer
Than the gangs that terrorized at school
Too far off to clearly see . . .
A boy with a sign hung
Round his neck, One Day Shot, was waved through
The barrier, his face masked in neon
As he hurried round the corner
Out of sight. I stared
At a recruiting poster, Uncle Sam's
Long bony finger a parody
Of Fate's: *Uncle Sam Wants You*!
                              And then, tear-shaped,
Pendulous, swelling, his bulk sagged into
Folds jiggling and rippling, a fat boy
Who'd washed out turned toward us
From the doctor and pressed
His sweating flesh flat

Against the glass: His shoulders heaved, sobs
Shook his chest and belly, a quiver
Like a shock—didn't I know him,
Glimpsed on my way to school
At daybreak or before, his face stung bright
By the frosted streetlight: Why should he weep, *weep*
To be rejected by the War?
We stood there paralyzed, a frieze of naked bodies
Straight-backed, swaybacked, torsos canted forward
Or swivelled at the hips, arms clutching
Ribcases or hung down at the sides, buttocks
Rounded or flat-cheeked, cocks drooped
And balls sagging, a sweat-pungent must
Permeating every corner . . .

I couldn't get my breath
And floated higher and higher, the neon
Buzzing in my eyes so brightly that the room
Dissolved to flesh restless and shifting, wave and wave
Of arms, heads bobbing, a surf of whispers,
"What's with this guy? what's wrong?"
Rising, rising—only the fat boy
Held steady in the room, his body an anchor
Pulling me back down, my air
Again swelling in my lungs: I stared into
His flesh, his cock nestled limply
Beneath the jut of his belly, his womanish
Breasts heaving with his sobs:
                              Wheezing
Asthmatically, weak-muscled, bone-thin,
I knew his shame as if he were my twin, his flesh
A rippling mirror I couldn't look away from
As I stood there waiting for my turn,
My heartbeat thudding louder, faster

—The doctor rose, waxen forehead shining, his hand
Reaching out, hovering near
The boy's arm, where it froze, almost touching:
For a long moment the boy's
Body hung there, hugging
The dull glass, gravidly afloat . . .
And then like a deep-sea diver, slowly, stiffly
He turned, his back walled against me, his separateness
Enclosing him thickly in his flesh
As aides crowded round, muscling him off.

Stone

Will, nerve, the stone heads of the kings of Judah—

in the basement of a dead prince's house,
they keep on living: faces worn
flat as a child's drawing, the bridge
of a nose missing, or an eye,
both eyes . . . Wrecked,
they're more themselves, a hall of giants
who in their heaviness seem happy, no regrets
about the losses that scrape
their faces bare to the neuter original
glare of quarried stone.

Everything in me that wears out—
more than body, will and nerve too—rests
in their ox-eyes dazedly staring forward;
thousand-years-old stoical, their thin worn lips say,
"If we're kings, what matter? We ended here
just like you, left dangling
at the far end of each other's gazes.
Stone? of course we're stone,
and no less so than when you stand there
thinking that if we'd been left

to sky and cloud, and not taken in
like beggars, rain would be cuffing
our faces even now . . . Our cheeks fretted
and stained, how irresistible
for eyes like yours
not to think of us as crying . . ."

Up close, each nick and scar
glares magnified all on its own
like lines of poems too natural ever
to be written, the raw, makeshift speech
of what the dead would say, like a child's
singsong, pidgin mother-tongue—
or else their mouths open wide
and they are lions on their pedestals
performing for every looker-on, more hustlers
than the leather boys
haunting Place Pigalle:

Stone heads, hard-headed stone, still living
on the love of the stone womb
which bore them, her maimed children
torn from their thrones by the Revolution's
angry hands . . . palms
soft against their rough cheeks
ripped and bleeding.

Intelligence

Wiretaps and tapes, concealed
bugs and mikes,
                    intercepted letters
full of passionate declarations, contradictory
intelligence—
                    how attached he'd grown
to the subject's documents, revising and rearranging
the influx of intelligence
with a sentiment, he acknowledged, almost
                    like love: he felt
the cool gray eyes of his superiors
trained on him, rebuking him
                    for swerving, for letting
himself go—such tender obsession
occasioned by the file!
                    Not quite the professional style
he or the Agency expected . . .

But such official loyalties
                    seemed mere protocol to this!—
what was wrong with him,
                    he wondered, that he construed

the documents to make the subject
seem a hero,

               a bastard whose sole patrimony
was a pair of shoes and a rusted sword
left by an unknown father beneath a stone?

And yet his exploits in the tabloids,
the headlines screaming,

SCOURGE OF MONSTERS STRIKES AGAIN!
HERO FOUNDS REPUBLIC

               were these heroic,
different in kind from the rumors,
unverified,

               of a rape, a murder?

—But to have met undisguised the devouring monster!
To have escaped the twisting tunnels of the maze . . .

On balance, for such a life,

               the hero's reputation wasn't bad:
think of the opportunities for evil

               a man of such qualities must have had!
How well he knew him—an essential innocence
that followed impulse, blind
to protocol, not noticeably more kind

               than he was cruel.
But to stamp *Case Closed* and cease

               gathering intelligence,
to give the hero up, almost, he admitted,
like a lover . . . :

               such limits the hero

unknowingly transgressed!
And the Agency, cold-blooded where
                limits were concerned ("mere protocol"?—
more like a second backbone!), committed
                to keeping order, could not afford
such sentiments—the Chief of Security
felt an awful pang: that the work of intelligence
                should lead to this . . .

He leaned back in his chair and sighed:
                a forged genealogy certifying
that the hero's father was a king; a mutual
assistance pact
                to aid in taking back the usurped crown:
he could see them now, the wind
blowing lightly, the two of them sweating
as they climbed the cliff, discussing
                the terms, exchanging information,
intelligence—
                how would his own face look
staring down across the sea
                as he gestured earnestly toward
some island, saying,
                "According to our sources,
the tax revenues . . ."
                And then, edging
the hero closer to the cliff, pointing
                out the harbor, he'd push.

The Wound

When I woke the darkness was so thick,
So palpable and black that my eyes
Seemed blind as stone staring into stone.

The blade that I had dreamed, efficient and quick
As it cut into my thigh, cleaning a gangrened
Wound infected to the bone, seemed poised

Above my throat: Close-grained, impenetrable,
The blackness rose before me like a wall.
And then off in the next room, nervous, light,

A soft padding as of an animal
Raced like my heartbeat in my temples
Round and round, trapped, stealthily desperate

As if hunting its own track, terrified
And captivated by its own odor.
Skin cool in the night air, eyes drilling

Through the dark, who I was before I
Slept had burned off like a vapor
So that amnesiac and pure, witnessing

My terror that I no longer recognized
As my own, my mind floated beyond me
To confront that frantic, closing footfall

As Jacob dreaming met his dark angel—
Though in my wrestling nothing blessed me
Or promised any blessing; but was a mask whose eyes

Were all black pupil, blind as molten tar.
I strained to see what paced there, my eyes burning
Through the dark until a pair of eyes blazed

Back across the blackness, an insistent, glazed
Staring that shimmered and disappeared.
The shining blade plunged at my throat, my mind

Stretched and twisted, its wires tightening
And turning as the creature lunged back and forth
And with a deep-throated yowling, thrashing

And thrashing to fight clear of its own circling,
Cleanly leapt away. I reached for the knife
But gripped only air, my eyes pressing

Deeper and deeper into the night's black stone,
Cutting the way the knife had cut into my wound,
Probing for the white shining of the bone:

What had I become? What darkness had my dream
Led me down into? Too frightened even
To move, I lay bound and sweating in

The sheets, the moon a warning-bell beating
On the glass, its light carving out the curtains
Like the shadow of a wing across the windowpane.

On the Seventh Floor: Cancer Ward

We are the elect in this inverse hell,
Souls lost to the traitor-temples of our bodies.
Familiars of the scalpel, confessors to our tumors,
We know we're dying faster, that each is delivered up

Into the talcummed hands of doctors who visit
Once a day while we smile our wooden smiles:
Our faces frame the question none of them will answer . . .
We are distracted from the truth

By the view of the highway twisting
Off between the hills. Sometimes waking,
I see the clouds lying like dark cattle
Asleep in the fields. Or see the cars

Slither head-to-tail, illumined
Through the fog's blur by the headlights'
Golden beams gilding what destinations,
What untouchable ends . . . But all of that goes on

Outside our days of routine pain. The nurses
Bring us morphine. Like a black, comforting spider
It spins a web around my brain.
The hypodermic's fang on which a drop

Colorless and odorless for a moment clings,
Is like the god I've dreamt who makes
His nightly rounds with a glowing piece of chalk—
He marks an X on my smock like a door . . .

We sit beneath the reading light that
At a finger's touch sends down its concentrated
Beam, a sword that lays its blade
On the common page we turn:

In the solitary hush
The white shoes whisper room to room
As word by word we lose our lives
In someone else's hope, another's pain.

The Seal

The mist was a face
Turned away from me
And the backwash along the cliff
A shout raised

In expectancy. I heard in ocean's
Chiding, salt-mouthed tones
The drawl and bitter deadpan
Of the prairie

And stood open to the wide light
Rebuking me: Bad blood
Ignored or spoken of
Too loudly, accents and intentions

Distorted or betrayed.
What reckoning kept nagging in my ear?
That the dead go on before us,
That we must meet them

Face to face?
And then I saw the seal,
His black sleek head
And raised intelligent eyes

As he bobbed and swayed,
A balance point
Among the waves,
And I heard a voice

Swimming counter
To that sea,
Unobliged to death
Or drab contingency:

"I shift my shape,
Am god or seal.
Ocean is my cowl
Whose boundless wash

Ministers to your finite wound.
My patience limns
The horizonless horizon.
The sun's ascension

Is my joy, the stars
The only net
To my possibilities.
Who you are

I do not care
But one glimpse of me
Can heal you:
Salt that smarts your eyes

Is only my element.
I see through ocean
As through a lens that sharpens
And magnifies,

And I see you too,
Poor forked thing,
No flippers
Or fluted tail:

If I could feel
The dash of pain
But I cannot
I might pity you."

Sun beating on the mist
Was like the iron lunge of bells,
Deliberate and distant,
Quickening and freshening:

Poised like the seal
Above the pouring tons
Of brine, I watched the dripping, diving
Head butt through the foam.

Fish Story

I was reading *Plutarch's Lives,* about the gods,
When I remembered someone I once knew, who came to our home
On Sundays for dinner with his girlfriend Kay;

She'd worked as a stitcher in a pillow factory
To send her previous boyfriend to school (he turned gay
Almost as soon as he got his degree, which maybe says something

About the way that books
Can reveal to people hidden parts of who they are);
He sat stiff and upright and talked about tuna-fishing,

How the deck gets slimy with scales,
And the sixteen-ounce steaks you eat morning, noon, and night,
And how you need that kind of nourishment

To gaff hundreds of fish and club them to death:
He talked about the blood, how it seeped
Even into your boots—and then he pulled up his pant-legs

And his socks were a pale pink
From the bloodstains, he said, but I didn't believe him,
A fish story, I thought, and shrugged . . .

But two years later I ran away from home
And went down to the docks to get on a boat,
Another longhaired, half-cocked kid with a yen for adventure:

They lay alongside each other like sleepers,
Bumping gently in the lazing swell,
Gulls screaming round the conning towers;

And in the hours I spent
Going boat to boat asking for the captains,
And when my back was turned being laughed at by the crews,

How I wanted to roll up my pants and show them
Blood-soaked socks, some badge or token
That I was more than what I seemed—

Though they were right to laugh, a landlubbing
Outsider, not knowing bow from stern, still too green
To tell a lie!—but what I started to say

About Plutarch and this guy: Plutarch speaks of
How the gods come down to us disguised,
And as I think about it now, on the docks that day

His pink socks shone in my mind's eye
As much an emblem as a thunderbolt or trident,
So that sometimes I wonder if he himself

Weren't a kind of god: He had the face
Of a sleepy animal, heavy lids and bushy hair and his eyes
Went blind when he talked, his spoon hesitating

Halfway to his mouth and the steam
Off the soup curling upward in the sunlight.
He talked about the death penalty as a good thing,

Which seems strange considering what later happened:
He was separated from his wife, with two kids,
When he'd met Kay, and one night, with a flensing knife,

He stabbed his wife twenty-seven times,
Face, throat, chest, back, stabbed her even in the eye
Like Marlowe. I was shocked when Kay told me,

But even more shocked when a big-time lawyer
Got him off with only six months in a work camp,
A temporary insanity plea, which I admit

Seems accurate, since afterward he turned
Himself in, not knowing exactly what he'd done,
But that there was blood all over him,

His face scratched and bleeding from her nails.
—He was definitely a god of some sort:
Deadpan, scary, though maybe not the worst,

For he took care of his own kids
And Kay's: His hand rested on the back of her neck
Pleased her, she nestled against that hand

Which seemed gentle and faithful that Sunday:
I see him like that, straight-backed in his chair,
Stonefaced as Ephesian Diana, her throat encircled

By a necklace of bulls' testicles, what poetic temperaments
Mistake for breasts!—I think of him at their wedding
Staring straight into Kay's eyes and her saying, "I do,"

The flashbulbs gasping in the startled air
And the air holding still as they drag out the kiss,
And then his hand clasped over hers on the cake knife.

four

Elk at Black Fork Canyon

Great furred noses nuzzling at hay bales,
Sidling jaws grinding the sweet
Green fodder, they looked up
To where I hunched, clutching

My coat tighter
As the cold like a mouth
Spoke promises.
Their eyes dark and wary

Stared through me as through crystal
And I dissolved into their looking
Like salt the long, liverish tongues
Licked from the block.

Staring from their eyes,
I bulked like a boulder,
A man-thing carved
Into the stone of the morning—

The mountain loomed into my eyes
Like a monstrous word
Pulverizing in its gutturals
The dwindling pebble

Of my name shouted down
The canyon. Trapped in the stillness,
The boulder-humped meadow, I heard
With more than, less than human ears

The cold mouth of the outdoors
Whisper me my wish:
Bone-trees sprouted
In mossy symmetry, skin

Coarsened with velvet fur,
And jaw and nose elongated
And snuffed the freezing air
With the cold scrutiny of a connoisseur.

My smell no longer wrinkled their nostrils
Or set their ears flapping, foolish,
But still lordly. Wholly animal,
My heart rose on knobbled

Legs lunging and stumbling
In the thicket of my chest
To the wild forebears, their heads lifting
Crowns of antlers—

Bursting in my ears, my name
Crashed back from the stillness
As beneath the unshod
Hooves the snow-crust

Cracked with frigid speed,
The wheeling, flicking tails
Unsheathed like skinning-knives.
They shied off down the canyon,

Disappeared into the beard
Of fog lengthening down the mountain,
The trampled snow spattered
Golden from their urine.

M. on Her Thirtieth Birthday

Sometimes I think I could be a yogi
And slow down my breath, the beating of my heart,
My blood as it goes around my body . . .
Haven't you sometimes felt like that, things start

To slow down until they almost stop?
When I was a girl I would walk the moors—
They're sort of bare and hilly, without
Trees—and imagine that Father and Mother

Would be gone when I got home, not dead
Exactly, just not there. Once it happened—
The house was dark. I listened and listened:
Two crows cawed, three hard cries, first one,

Then the other, and finally together,
A black sharp sound that rang inside my ears
The way things ring when you've been struck. The floor
Creaked when I sat down at the piano,

Not frightened, but expectant. The crows, silent,
Made the first note seem so loud I couldn't
Believe it would ever fade, it rang out
So clearly, so sure against the quiet.

I pressed the hold pedal and with the flat
Of my palm cuffed the keys. The notes trembled
Together, the overtones mounting, the flats
Indistinguishable from the sharps, a wall

Of rising sound pitched higher and higher
And I felt happy, but sad that I could feel . . .
Feel happy—what I mean is that I was sure
They would have punished me, just a lot of jangle,

No tune or anything to steer by . . .
Now both of them are dead, Father ten years,
Mother twenty. I guess that's what it means to be
Grown up, to know you wished them gone, and now they are.

Don't Go to the Barn

for my mother

The brick of the asylum shimmered in the sun
As I watched the black hood of your depression
Lower down across your face immobile
But for the eyes staring off into the crystal

Blue bracing the scorched mountain.
Fire like a razor had swept the rock face clean . . .
Cut off from your despair, I stared across the lawn
To your drug-blinkered gaze staring down

The shivering, flashing eyes of the aspen:
Blinking back that glare, I saw your heart eaten
By the gloom of the weather-warped barn
Off behind the orchard alleys convulsing

Into bloom, saw you walk into the shudder
Of blossoms rippling down in spasms
Of cool wind, the weeds you tread under
Springing back bristling, the tough, fibrous green

Closing in behind you, the chill brushings
Of the leaves feathering dew across your skin.
The barn like a gray flame burns above the bloom,
The hoof-cratered mud, glistening in the sun,

Squelching as you slog across the yard.
And now you enter into the raftered
Damp of lofty spaces cut by the veer
And slice of scaly wings, knot the knot hard,

Loop the rope around the beam, the zero
Of the noose dangling down: Your gaze swings
To mine, and I see your chances narrow:
Sprawled on the table, the volts axing

Through your skull, you jerk and shake,
Your body drugged to flab trembling and trembling,
Your teeth clenching jolt after jolt until crackling
In your brain a voice of fire speaks,

Divinely disapproving: "Don't go to the barn
And try to hang yourself. Don't go to the barn
And try to hang yourself. Don't go to the barn
And try to hang yourself. Rose, don't go to the barn."

A Vision

The year I had my operation I
Thought that I would die. You were off in Spain,
Living, as you put it, "in a cheap pension
With a view of a steam shovel and the sea."

That was the summer your brother "saw God"
(Like mother like son) and sat doing nothing,
Staring, thinking, listening to the windchime
Ringing and ringing. As a child he was so good—

Too good, obviously. When the hospital
Released him, he came home for a while,
Home, to us, to what we'd been and done . . .
He told me he had the power of healing

In his hands, which were clasped around his knees
The way he used to as a child—he looked away
As he said it, ashamed and afraid
When I asked him to heal me. The blood

Burned in my cheeks when he apologized . . . Once,
When madness meant the fits my dolls would throw,
I had a vision. I was on my way to get the cows,
And dust, lifting at each step, hovered in soft puffs

Around my ankles until I couldn't see
My feet as if between me and the ground
Were high-piled clouds moving slowly, steadily
To a collision. I was certain

That if I turned I'd see in place of town
Nothing—no church, no school, no grain elevator—
Just an empty sweep of prairie rippling
With heat waves in the afternoon shimmer,

The distance curdled into crawling sheets
Of water that gleamed and trembled in the air . . .
I was scared inside my head, as if a stranger
Thought my thoughts. I crossed my fingers, shut

My eyes, and said a charm—but when I opened them,
The shock kept me from glancing round: Thunderheads boiled
Up and blocked the sun—and I saw it, crumpled
In the lane. The mother kept grunting

And nuzzling at its shoulder, grunting
And nuzzling and shoving. The legs were stiff—
It had been dead for hours—the belly puffed
Up to bursting like a balloon. . . . It all seems wrong

When I think of it now—I'd seen dead things, wrung
A rooster's neck, watched it reel around the yard
In immense, drunken rings. It was the tongue,
Swollen, clamped between the jaws, the odd

Look it had beneath the clots of flies, the way
It flickered and crawled and seemed to hum
Not a tune exactly, but like a tune,
The notes of a tune you can't brush away,

That hums itself over and over in your mind—
What was wrong that my thoughts kept chasing round and round?
I knew the humming was the flies, that the cows
Were ordinary, cud-chewing cows,

That the cows and flies were just cows and flies . . .
I thought of a music-box, how it tinkles
Faster and faster the quicker you turn the handle,
Tumbling everything together, the cows, the flies . . .

The thunderheads heaped higher. The storm broke—
Everything was rain, no cows, no flies;
I stood there, blinking, woozy, weirdly happy—.
Jolts of lightning shivered down my neck

And burned all around me like the razor strop
That flickered in the dark of the tractor shed
Where they punished us kids for acting up
—And then I heard a voice that made me want to hide,

Muttering things as it gasped and slurred—
Crude things, you know what I mean—like my father's
Voice when he got stonefaced drunk or mad . . .
I told no one, and even if I had

(In those days there was nobody to tell),
How could I have known that the girl I was
Would grow up into what I am and pass
That to my sons, "visions" and all.

How far-off and strange she seems, that girl.

Premonition

Your girdles, wigs, your stretchmarked flesh turned out
Into that wilderness of corridors
That led you and your fellow wanderers
To the short-circuiting of your despairs
—Distances that would not bring you near
Wiped from my eyes your red-faced tears, your fits
Of anger and religious terror.
Blind to your desolate stare at supper,
I ate, slept, my coherent miseries
Making me competent with pain, the future . . .
My child's eyes, grown larger than the years,
Stare into your madness like a mirror:
What was it you saw when you looked at me,
Your soap-slimed hands churning underwater?

Animus

A face, my face, stares back from glass pocked
By midnight rain. But it is not my face at all,
But a woman's face, dangerous, spiteful, and unforgiving.
What have I done to deserve a look like that?
With a swivel of my chair, I could make her disappear—
But I meet her stare. Behind her, as if they were bloody thoughts,
A jungle of roses blooms and blooms, climbing the fence
Toward the thunder-heaped air flashing and rumbling.
Is this the sister in me coming out, not pretty, not devoted,

But wild? She is obviously impossible;
Or perhaps she's ill with some secret and hates me
For not finding out, for not rummaging my mind
Like a dead man's closet, airless and too close.
I confess I am blind to her obsession—
She mocks me with my own earnest look, lips pursed, sympathetic.
She is maddeningly silent, this woman. She refuses to complain,
To explain the storm's tears spattering on her face,
As if the dark held an infant in its cradling arms,

One that can't keep from weeping.
Her will must be iron to stand up to such grief—
I would melt in a minute, but she hovers unmoved,
Meeting my eyes unflinchingly as an animal's.
Each drop stings, scouring her cheeks,
But all she does is stare, beyond turmoil or fear—
Her gaze like a mirror grips me tight, tight:
I am the one losing heart, her soul moving into mine,
Leading my gestures, my expressions—and now my thought:

I cannot look away, for what she thinks, I am . . .
She smiles, shaking out her electrifying hair,
And I lean closer and closer to the glass.
I can almost hear her whisper, like water trickling
Through the roses, each drop balancing on the petals
Like a word she lets drop, drop into the trough
Of stillness and blindness between flashes—
I feel my heart open to enclose that welling salt
As the drops, bright, blood-warm, streak the glass.

You Have Her Eyes

for my mother

Note and note your fingers play and bring me
Pale face to face with that self-sufficing boy
I was at eight or nine. How earnest, frail,
And driven he now seems, the scales
Mechanically repeating and repeating
With the harsh innocence of practicing

And you the tall presence, even when absent,
The keys ring out to, clumsily chromatic
Or climbing bravely until the thumb tucks
Under and stumbles. You look
Up and I see you see me in the mirror,
Your grown-up child, and the melody falters,

The quavering hymn your mother used to sing,
Out of the ivory palaces, into a world of woe . . .
Do you see that I see you faintly smiling,
Absorbed in the echo
Of the overtones, your wrists delicately cocked?
And now your hands drop and, murmuring, you look

Into the soft dazzle of the keys, the gloss
And swirl of the grain. I hear her voice,
Reedy, thin, echo over yours as you whisper
The refrain; and see the shimmer,
Distant, unreachable in the glass,
As you raise your eyes and our looks cross.

Last Wish

for my grandmother

The cars flashed like scales as the hearse-headed snake
Crawled down the dusty lane to the funeral tent
Flapping dove-gray wings in the wind-stropped heat.
I saw you snug in the hearse's air-conditioned gut

And imagined your eyes opening, peering
Through the cloud of velvet lining the brass lid,
Your thunder-gray pupils laconically resigned:
Dead or alive, your shrug, half-humorous, meant

More than your dull kiss: Frail as a baby bird,
Bald head swaddled in a red bandanna,
You craned forward, bared your gums, the words slurring
Round your exasperated, morphine-crippled tongue:

"Make sure they read Ecclesiastes,
'Vanity, saith the preacher, all is vanity.'
What your granddad didn't waste getting cross-eyed drunk
I've squandered on the library. I know more folks

In the graveyard than I do today in town."
Your skull shone like a parable too simple
To understand as you licked your blistered lips
And motioned for the ice chips I fed you from

A spoon, your eyes, sly and daring, risking mine:
"Don't overdo it with the tears and such.
I've left you your granddad's broken pocket-watch,
The Santa Fe Special with the gold-plate back?

Remember the seashells in the box upstairs
And you can take your pick of the photographs.
And do what your granddad said the day before he died,
'Go out and get yourself a girl as good as mine.'

Now there was a man who had no use for books—."
And shrugging off the flush tinging your gray cheek:
"But what he lacked in brains he made up in looks."
And staring straight through me: "You ought to write a poem."

The Root Cellar

A slithering rustle through ivy and leaves
Like the voice of a dead one returning:
Again that gone sweetness pours in my ear
And leads me back down the lightless stairs
To the cobwebbed dank of the root cellar,
Underworld of onions, beets, potatoes
Shrouded in burlap's rough puckers and folds.
Your voice exhumed from the swallowing sod
Gathers breath, freshens: My tongue cleaves to yours
As we snake in and out of the old tune's
Stinging whiplash of notes, your alto twang
Upstaging my tenor as you brandish
An onion like an apple: My mouth waters
For the sweet white flesh stinging my eyes to tears.

Vows

The cracked creekbed sang with heat that afternoon.
My eyes scoured the brush for shed snakeskin
When far off the dazed whistle of a train
Woke in me your sighing
In the close bedroom where I watched your chest
Heave, swilling the dead air.
Your wedding photograph
Stared stiff-faced from the dresser
As immaculate in your tight black shoes
And vest, your youth havocked with the worn face
That was Grandfather. Dawnlight
Razoring through cracks in the shutters
Chattered on your false-teeth gleaming in a jar . . .

How unreal to know you those fifty years ago,
Your shambling red-faced innocence as you waltzed
Her round the yard, her hard
Unpracticed kiss smearing lipstick on your cheek
As you drove off waving from the stove-pipe-black Ford
That racketed and jolted across the rutted prairie,
The tin cans strung from the axle
Dolefully clattering, your dusty trail hovering
And drifting in the glare . . . Was it you,

Grandfather, sweet-talking and vigorous,
Your barrel-chested glamor
Swelling your pinched black suit, the swagger
Of your tenor upstaging her thin soprano
As you "raised Cain" at the socials,
Your whooping, blear-eyed bravado
Outfacing her cool stare? Through trembling veils
Of heat I see you take her hand,
Your bluff face peering intently across the plain,
The junipers' long shadows
Weaving among the guests gravely listening
To the vows on your dry halting lips.
The rich brown ooze of White Woman Creek
Gasps and sighs behind you in the sun lazily exploding
Above heat-tranced fields of grain, the air's
Cloud-piled acres
Tumbling and billowing . . .

Grandfather, antiquated harvester,
How you chortled and choked
As you chugged the burlap jug, then snaked
Your noon cigar around my head,
Claiming "like the devil" to blow smoke
From your foxed pupils. I drank in
Your bourbon breath as you sat me in your lap
And plowed down the rasping stubble,
The dust-drenched umbrella louring above our heads,
Our brilliant red bandannas
Pulled up to our eyes
As we swatted and swatted the butting flies . . .
Toiling and faithful as the old John Deere,
How you endured, your fire-tongued
Credo, "Plow straight, plow straight" hissing

And scorching like a love-word in my ear . . . I see you
Tranced and hieratic in your dust-stung goggles,
Looming above the tractor fouled
In fuming clouds of oil, the motor mumbling
And snorting as you gouge the fallow soil,
The harrow disks glinting through fresh-turned loam,
The seed drilled
Into steaming, stretchmarked ground . . .

Grandfather, like a heat wave you shimmer
At the edge of thought, a breath, a world
Away, your absences that come so near
Rekindling the withered junipers, the whirl
Of locusts that wheezing dawn
When glazed with fever and morphine
You turned from the flowers
Perjuring the stench of your gangrene
And met that pared-down grin,
Its deadpan glare
Grimacing at the dust-motes that swirled
Like screens sheltering your pain. Betraying
Your labored breath, I nodded reassurance
Until you waved me off, eyes straining
From the sockets as you saw through me
To your death: After an hour's
Delirious mumbling about
"That hailed-out section north of town,"
You gummed an awful thumbs-down grin, Beechnut
Staining brown your chin
As you spat in the rust-eaten coffee can
And shrugged back, eyes open, to your pillow.

The Last Word

for Lem

As if your half-witted tongue
Spoke with an eloquence
Death bestows, I heard your voice
Muffled through the dark
Layers of cemetery loam:

"They found me black-suited
In the shuttered half-dark, my eyes
Dug like claws into the clouds'
Soft feather-turnings. What kept me
Separate the broiling sun

Of intellect now shone on fiercely:
In the sheep-pens stinking
Of dung and lanolin,
I buried my face in the ewe's
Swollen side and listened

For the lamb the way
The night sky listens
To the synapse-fire
Of meteors, the fibrillating
Heartbeat of the stars.

I heard the cells crackle
Into being, the embryonic
Brain begin to burn:
Hunger. Thirst. Beneath my ear
My own disastrous birthing,

The umbilicus strangling
Like a whip around my neck,
Shoved through the momentary
Breach memory tore open—
Dying revealed to me my birth,

How half my brain went dark,
One side of a universe
Pinched out like a candle:
Just smart enough to sense
My difference, yet not know why—

Even my death was the thrust
Of a bewildering punchline: On Thanksgiving
Morning mouthwatering
Pain shoved like a spit
From my bowels to my brain."

Hope

for Aunt Hope

Overhung by evergreen, your house was cool
Those afternoons the sun's long ghost shimmered
In the fading curtains. The rocker's senile
Back and forth wore ruts in the floor, the boards'

Soft creaking wheezing in, out. It's seven years
Since I saw you last for the last time,
Your eyes molten with remembrance's flicker
As events like magma poured and cooled, time

Confounding my grown-up face with your image
Of the photogenic, faded child.
Who was I to you?, your bed barred like a cage,
A stainless-steel cradle, as in your head

My name roamed connectionless. And you too
Were strange, your hip smashed, your legs drawn up
And shrunken like a cricket's, your eyes' blue
Like clouded water in which I saw trapped,

Lost in terminal helplessness, the eyes
Of my aunt of childhood, ironic, clear,
And merciless, their killing-with-kindness
Stare that sent me to the boneyard hour after hour

Those endless afternoon wars at dominoes
Still lurking aloof from your stranger's face.
I held your hand and saw in the window
The two of us suspended beyond the glass

As through us waved a dusty branch, a rag
Of green wiping our smudge of color
From the air. . . . Seven years, and your name still drags
Its luminous syllable like a lure

My heart still swallows, open-mouthed and hungry,
Its barb of light irresistible:
"Go fish in the boneyard," I hear you say,
Your eyes poker-faced, impenetrable.

The Porch Swing

The chains creak and creak
As they used to when I swung in the porch swing
Back and forth, and listened to the mourning doves
Buried in the green of the pines. How far
That odd, rippling call traveled then, droning
On and on through the lazy, sun-doused Sunday, call
Trailing call serenely through the noon
And afternoon. In the shade under the eaves
Two sets of swallows chittered above the air-conditioner
Dripping in a rusty, oblong pan, their blue-gray feathers
And clay-daubed nests gathering against them
The glare of the heat waves
Rising through the warping pine-shadows
That wove and wove through the patchy grass.

My legs, once so short
That I'd lunged back and forth
To make the swing take off
And float like a rocketship off among the stars,
Were far too long to do anything with but tuck beneath the seat
And drag the toes of my shoes against the cracked concrete.

How changed and not changed it all seemed
—And yet impossible to imagine anyone had lived there,
The blinds drawn back on her living room
Loud with conversing great-aunts and distant cousins,
The murmur of mourning crepe swaying easy in the heat
While the strict, tall hall-clock's
"Tick tick tick" measured the shining interval
Each pearl-buttoned shoe stepped through,
Her gloved hand's electric touch, the elect
Fingers shimmering in silk,
Absently stroking, wholly casual, the prickling nape
Of her great-nephew's neck. How much given
That will never be gotten back!
An alp of sheeted furniture, a feather-duster
Aloof on a loop of wire, a box of shells nestled
In tissue paper, all of it reckoned up, all of it there,
Still to be disposed of, finally put out of sight.
And yet voluble, inevitable
As the doves' lazing moans, among the chittering
Of the swallows, the creaking of the chains, their voices
Talk on and on through the long afternoon,
Dizzying, constant as the sway of the swing:

"We had moisture down south." "The White Woman
Rose six inches—." "If the price keeps going down . . ."
"Hailstones bigger than your fist!"
And beneath the pock-faced uncle
Talking cheerful smut, the tight-faced, calculating,
Chainsmoking aunt who wept too much, prayed too much,
A long, audible sigh, gentler, grieving, wondering at grieving:

"You miss them, and then you don't. Your Aunt Hope,
She was a beauty. There were many girls
Not so pretty who found a husband. She lived with her Dad
On the homestead after her mother died,
And then she took care of Lem,
The half-wit brother. We used to garden together,
She and I. She was elected forty years straight
To the Courthouse Registry, and then—she lost her memory.
Folks hated to vote her out, but she kept misplacing deeds . . .
You know she once christened a battleship?
She was the nearest living relation;
They flew her to San Francisco in '43, oh, '44,
To launch the USS *Owen*.
This photograph's her holding up the magnum
—You can see just how pretty—and here, this one's
Of the layer cake we baked for her retirement party."

Sunday Drive

Beyond the window fields of milkweed pass.
The engine's hum and the spinning wheels beneath
Are like the drone of far-off voices
In the front seat. He sees in the glass

The hover of the peaks and his own face
Skimming across the darkness. Shadows
Sliding off the slopes lift up the Queen Anne's lace
Buoyant as the stars above the meadows'

Rising mists. The face that speeds along beside
Meets his wide stare (eyes of a schoolteacher,
Eyes of a scientist?). The distant glide
Of all the stars is entrusted to his care

As he voyages out among them, connecting
Them like numbered dots in a puzzle book.
Those three stars make the belt of Orion,
And sequestered over there in a nook

Next to the moon the Seven Sisters shine.
He can almost hear them talk, their glimmering
Like whispers of what he will become
(Scientist like dad; schoolteacher like mom?).

The round world spinning spins beneath the tires
Till the dry fields borne along on rivers
Of white mist seem to float in a blur
Through the face looking in as if the fields were

Dreams dreamed till they came true. The road
Spinning faster catches up to the tires
That slow to a standstill beneath the turning stars.
His eyes slowly close on the eyes of the world.